END OF.

ASH FLANDERS

CURRENCY PRESS
The performing arts publisher

GRIFFIN
THEATRE
COMPANY

CURRENT THEATRE SERIES

First published in 2022
by Currency Press Pty Ltd,
PO Box 2287, Strawberry Hills, NSW, 2012, Australia
enquiries@currency.com.au
www.currency.com.au

in association with Griffin Theatre Company.

Typeset by Brighton Gray for Currency Press.
Cover features Ash Flanders; photo by Pia Johnson; design by Alphabet.

Currency Press acknowledges the Traditional Owners of the Country on which
we live and work. We pay our respects to all Aboriginal and Torres Strait
Islander Elders, past and present.

A catalogue record for this
book is available from the
National Library of Australia

Contents

End Of. was first produced by Darebin Arts Speakeasy at Northcote Town Hall on 11 March 2020, with the following cast:

ASH   Ash Flanders

Director, Stephen Nicolazzo
Set and Costume Design, Nathan Burmeister
Lighting Design, Rachel Burke
Sound Design, Tom Backhaus
Stage Manager/Operator, Alyssa Hill

CHARACTER

ASH, an angry, insolent man, trapped somewhere between the petulance of youth and the bitterness of old age.

This play text went to press before the end of rehearsals and may differ from the play as performed.

ASH: 'Do you agree the time is now ten-thirty-eight a.m. by my watch?'

I've started this new job where I transcribe police interviews and that's always the cops' first move, getting the suspect to agree they're in the same time. In playwriting we call this 'world-building', establishing the world of the characters and the rules for the audience. Only, the audience in this case is incredibly small, it's just me. And the world of the characters is an interrogation room, two police officers, one suspect and a video camera recording the whole thing. A very cheap show if you're thinking of rounding out your season. Although I can already hear you saying, 'Does it have to be two cops? Make it one and we'll consider it for twenty-twenty-three.' The recording needs to be transcribed for the prosecution and defence. Basically, the entire legal system depends on me—and people like me—and our ability to sit at a desk and slowly type out everything said in that room.

This is my first regular job since I wore fangs in a theatre restaurant and it's great because I'm essentially dealing with the same people. The only real difference is I'm used to working in places that have identities—cabaret venues, gay bookstores, theatres—places that loudly scream who and what they are, usually empty. The only identifiable thing in this whole place is on the ground floor, a Hudsons Coffee, where I spend ten minutes every morning waiting for an elderly man to make my vanilla latte.

And then I take that vanilla latte and I ride up to level nine where I land at Stark and Landon, which for all I know could be named after its founders or washes of denim. I didn't do a lot of research on the place, I got the job through a friend who said, 'It's the perfect place for a creative to work, Ash, every day is something new. You'll get so much strong material out of it.' Which was very attractive to me. In public I spend most of my time ignoring whoever I'm with in order to listen in on everyone else and now I was finally being paid to eavesdrop?! It sounded too good to be true! Which of course it was when I learned, after taking the job, that I'd earn better money making vanilla lattes downstairs.

The office is … just like any other office. Although I'd wager this one's a little more dystopian because aside from the typical rows of cubicles, the grey carpet and the water cooler, all the employees at Stark and Landon wear these colossal headphones that make us look surgically attached to our computers. Occasionally when your ears get overheated, or more likely overwhelmed by the sound of a Bendigo ice lord losing his mind, you take off the headphones and the world outside is blissfully quiet. No-one talks at Stark and Landon. Ever. The only sound you hear is the clack clack clacking of keys. At first the sound was soothing, almost meditative, but one day I imagined a thousand monkeys at a thousand typewriters and I started to wonder whether life as a chimp was really worth it for some strong material.

The audio is controlled by a pedal underneath your desk. It's like we're all are operating sewing machines, which I'll admit does give the place a fun, sweatshoppy vibe. Push your foot down and the audio plays. Take it off and the audio stops and automatically steps back three seconds so you're ready to hear the same thing again. And again. And again. There are two kinds of pedals: the old ones, which are good, and the new ones, which are bad. I have a new one which needs to be unplugged and then plugged back in so it works. I'm okay with this—it means I get to take off the headphones, I get to stand up, I get to stretch my legs—as if every day is now a long-haul flight. But it's started to affect my productivity.

You see, the work day is itemised, atomised and metricised down to the last second and it's crucial everyone sticks to the system. As soon as you complete a transcript you do your page count and your word count. You then enter that data into an application so the company knows how long the work has taken you. That is then averaged out over a month to give you your page-count-per-hour. Every employee must complete a minimum of seven pages per hour and a higher page count means you might graduate from the entry-level pay rate, level one.

On my first day on the job I was given a tour of the office by the man who hired me, James. 'That's the computer, that's the toilet.' But before he left he gave me a word of warning, 'There are some people that have worked here for years and never made it off level one, don't let that happen to you.' He sounded more disgusted in them than by the sex offenders he made his living from. A month later he reappeared at my desk.

'Hey, Ash, I was just going through your productivity report and I couldn't help but notice you'd signed out of a job but didn't clock out of work for another six minutes. Do you have any idea what you were doing with all that time?'

All that time.

'I don't know, James, I think I was taking a shit. Too many vanilla lattes, you know?' I was trying to shock him into some humanity, or at least remind him of mine. 'Yeah, I thought that might be it. Just remember you should always do that stuff before you sign out of a job. Okay. It might be too much milk, don't forget we've got a kitchenette full of Nescafé, help yourself. Anyway, I'll let you get back to it, I don't wanna slow you down.'

I haven't seen him since.

Any pride I took in being a writer vanished just as quickly. You see, writing isn't creative at Stark and Landon, it's just as systemised. A sentence must always be followed by a double space. A sentence cannot end with the word 'like'. 'O.K.' is spelled with two capital letters and two full stops. And while 'and so' can go together 'so and' requires a hyphen in between because it's clearly a change of thought. But hyphens can also be used for compound adjectives, common words we type like passenger-side window or sawn-off shotgun. And the wily hyphen is also used to represent repetitions—like, like, you know, you know. Actually 'like' and 'you know' rarely need hyphens, they're often 'nested' between two commas like the word 'yeah' because, yeah, they don't, you know, change the meaning of the, like, sentence.

All good writing has structure but the reason I struggle so much with this job is that it's all structure and no expression, like the building itself. See, I want to write how the person tells their story. When you hear a man explain that he just stabbed his best friend, who was the best man at his wedding, in order to steal his power tools to buy drugs and as he's filling the bag he hears his friend—who survived—literally pulling an et tu Brutus, 'Why, Chooka? Why?' you gotta treat this material with the respect it deserves! Give me some commas, unleash the exclamation mark, let me at least put a few words in italics or the guy we cast as Chooka will be useless! You don't let the characters write themselves, it'd be a mess, let me just punch it up a little.

That's when the friend who got me the job—and who is now my manager, correcting my transcripts—reminds me of the stakes involved.

'This is for court, Ash. Someone could hang for this.'

Such is life.

Another really frustrating part of this job is that people don't speak in complete sentences. Ever. Just another way real life is in no way like the stories we tell ourselves—or the one you're watching right now. In real life we fall down rabbit holes. We obsess over a minor detail or we start to retract the thing we thought we wanted to say in the first place. But mostly we just can't be bothered to finish a thought. We're a lot more scattered, messy and inconsistent than stories suggest. And you're even more scattered when the police just busted you for carjacking or you were found naked in the Deniliquin Newsagency.

Truth is, I used to speak incredibly badly.

Eugh!! Eargh!! That's me at eighteen months old asking for a drink, with tears running down my face, begging my family to understand me. Soon I'll be taken to a paediatrician who will identify that I'm mostly deaf due to large blockages in my ears. He'll operate, the world of sound will open up, and for the first time in my life I'll hear the voices of my family. Only, now we have a new problem. The way thought and language interacts means that while I now have an abundance of thoughts to share, I have no real road map of how to do it. I want to finish a thought, I want to get to the end of a sentence, but I can never seem to find my way there. Everything sort of spills out everywhere all at once, like a flash flood or a Courtney Love interview. After five more years enjoying this adorable personality quirk, my dad will insist that I see a speech pathologist. I don't want to brag but compared to my two siblings I have required the most in terms of specialist care.

My mother, Heather, was having none of it. Sure, they couldn't make sense of what I was saying, but was any of it going to be that interesting anyway? I was a child, she'd lost interest the second I developed free will. But she sat with me, a study in resentment, as the therapist got me to visualise a gently flowing river.

'Now, Ashleigh, let your thoughts float down the river, that's it, nice and gently, all in one direction.' Mum thought the whole thing was a scam but according to Flanders family lore I came out of that room speaking perfectly and—better yet—they never had to shell out for a second appointment. Only once in this job have I had a suspect speak in full, complete sentences. It was wonderful. 'Finally,' I thought, 'Someone from my team!' He was being arrested for child pornography.

That's the thing. You develop a real gallows humour at a place like Stark and Landon. I mean, how else can you respond when you hear a man say 'I knew this would be a bad year once they found those maggots in my foot'? Newbies like me typically go through a baptism of fire with their first few horrific cases—I mean, it can be heartbreaking to see the bad choices people make—and slowly the humour forms around the transcriber like a suit of armour. But growing up in my family, laughing at others was a sign of great breeding and so I arrived not just in a suit of armour but riding a giant indestructible zeppelin of sick humour.

The zeppelin was constructed somewhere in that hazy five-year period—ooh, compound adjective, five-year period—between being able to hear properly and being able to talk properly. I'm sat in the family car, a white 1986 Mitsubishi Nimbus, trapped in the back with my younger sister, Erin. My brother, Jeremy, eight years older than me—and he'll never let any of us forget it—is in the front seat opposite Mum and ash from her cigarette keeps flying back and hitting me in the face. A few years later one of Erin's friends will complain of being quite badly burned only to have my mother say, 'GET OVER IT OR GET OUT, END OF.'

I'm beyond used to the ash at this point. In fact, I'm pretty sure I only got my name because Heather was actually calling for the ashtray. I wipe my face and try to catch her eye. I wait until we're stopped at a light and I stare into the mirror while letting my body go limp and crossing my eyes. I agree, not very sophisticated, but when you can't talk properly you really rely on facial tricks for attention. Besides, I know she hates this.

'STOP THAT! PEOPLE WILL THINK YOU HAVE SPECIAL NEEDS!' Only you know in the eighties that's not quite the language she used. 'SO WHAT IF THEY DO?! WHAT IF THEY DO THINK I HAVE SPECIAL NEEDS AND ... AND ... '—only

I can't finish the thought, which, depending on how you look at it, either strengthens or weakens my argument.

'Jesus Christ,' she says as the lights change and another cigarette is lit. And that's when Jeremy leans over and says something, something I can't quite make out and suddenly she's laughing. No, not laughing, cackling. My mother cackles like the grandest of grand high witches. And she looks beautiful when she laughs, I think along with the drinking and the smoking it's just what her body was meant to do. The laughter possesses her. It's explosive and raw and I immediately see it as the highest praise you can attain. That's what I want. So I sit back and uncross my eyes and as the two Jeremys merge back into one I stare at the back of his head, this brother who can make magic like this happen on command. And like a Shakespearean villain or—to be honest, any middle child—I vow that I will become better than him at this and take my rightful place at the front of the Nimbus.

Because I will be funny, Jeremy.

Oh, yes.

I will make her laugh.

At least that's my version of events. Ask Jeremy and he'll have another story and, yeah, you probably would laugh more at his. The truth isn't fixed, it all depends where you're sat in the Nimbus, which is why so much time is spent in these interviews getting the suspect to stand by one version of events. We even have these keyboard shortcuts for the common things police say to force a suspect to commit to a narrative.

'So you're telling us that,' 'Would you agree,' 'Is it fair to say,' 'Just to confirm,' which is followed by the confirmation afterwards, oddly almost always a triple-hitter, 'Okay, yeah, all right,' 'Yeah, all right, no worries,' 'Of course, all right, mate.'

But this way of talking, another system within a system within a system, means that the more time I spend at Stark and Landon the less original, the less zany, the less funny it all seems. Every day feels pre-written, automated, like the pedal I push that takes me nowhere. It's the same story, it's the same interview, it's the same vanilla latte, again and again and again.

And there are days when I have written twelve thousand words. Twelve thousand words. That's a whole play. That's this play! And

I've written it in one day like I heard Noël Coward could do, only my play has no wit, no sophistication and worst of all I'm legally forbidden from ever performing it—which is why everything I said before was strictly hypothetical.

This is the only excuse I have for my latest unproductive work habit—reading old scripts I wrote with my writing partner, Declan. I mean, it's incredibly embarrassing that I do this, but it's the truth. The fixed truth. And I've been drawn to our really old stuff when we wrote just for the joy of it. A time when time wasn't something you measured, because it was infinite.

▼ ▼ ▼ ▼ ▼

It's 2007. Declan and I are driving over the Westgate Bridge in search of a bloody solution. Our latest—and second—show together culminates in a drag queen stabbing herself to death because she's being psychically controlled by one of her twin albino children. Suffice to say, we knew this moment called for greater emotional truth than tomato sauce or ice-cream topping. No, we needed blood. And more importantly, we needed gore. And being the imaginative artists that we are, we knew an ingenious hack for human organs—animal organs.

After calling several butchers and learning they're no longer legally allowed to sell offal, one man said it might be worth calling a knackery. Now, I'd never heard that word before, so Declan—who's rurally intelligent—told me a knackery was a butcher, typically of horses. They're unregulated and because the meat isn't sold for human consumption they're as wild and free as the steeds they slaughter.

We arrived at a nondescript, well, shack, off an industrial road in Altona Meadows and both sat in my car, each refusing to move, vainly hoping the other one would get out and deal not only with the blood and the gore but with the incredibly macho men who made their living by literally killing beauty. I tried to butch up my look in the mirror but an off-the-shoulder top is fruity no matter how flat you make your hair and so I decided to plead my case. 'Hey, since I'm a vegetarian, would you mind if I just stayed in the car? Besides, I drove so … '

It wasn't much of a battle to be honest. Some innate part of Declan was being called to the killing floor and in a matter of seconds he was happily trotting off like many a doomed Clydesdale. Only, now I was all by myself in the middle of nowhere—and if you know Altona Meadows you know I'm not exaggerating. And I started to panic. What if they were playing some sort of sick homophobic prank on him? What if they were forcing him to kill a horse himself as some sort of payment? What if the whole thing was a front and Declan was already a sex slave, just another country boy taken in by the bright lights of big-city knackery? Sick with worry, I waited just twenty more minutes before bravely stepping out of my Barina and into the unknown.

It was dark inside. And hot. It was exactly what you think a temple of murder would look and smell like. Everything felt … a little too close. Thankfully, Declan was all right. In fact, he was having a great time considering there was an entire skinned horse at his feet, slowly bleeding out over a steel grating. Apparently when he'd arrived and told the man who he was, the knackerer had simply walked over to the skinned horse, grabbed a large knife and sliced its belly wide open. 'It was shocking how quickly everything spilled out, Ash.'

At our feet were yellow organs, purple organs, everything still connected, they looked like they were still pulsing they were so fresh. Declan and I didn't say a word—we were both thinking the exact same thing—how did we get so lucky? Declan began pointing out the bits we wanted while the knackerer cheerfully waded through the innards and bagged everything up. It was an Easter-egg hunt for psychopaths! As we waved goodbye I noticed the bag starting to sweat on the inside from the heat. The only thing more shocking was the grin on Declan's face. Because we did it! We were going to have actual animal organs onstage at La Mama, Carlton! And better yet, our showbag was free!!!

But as we drove back across the Westgate I started to understand the true cost of the bag. It wasn't the smell of sweet success that filled our nostrils, but rather the rotted stink of horse death. We cracked a window, focused on the driving, thinking only of the reaction this stunt was going to get. But even that image of a sold-out La Mama thirty-person standing ovation couldn't compete with the rancid stench of equicide by the time we finally got to his house in Brunswick.

'Hey, maybe we should wash these?' he said and so we washed the entrails in the way men wash everything, by leaving them to soak in a sink while we did other things. The afternoon was spent on admin for the show, opening-night guest list, and chasing up all the taxidermy we could now afford since our special effects were 'in-kind'.

Before I left I took one last look in the sink. 'Hey, is that just … shit?' We thought about it for honestly far too long for people claiming to be university educated before concluding that, yes, since those were intestines, that sink now housed an entire equine digestive tract, from grass to ass. This time I pulled out the big guns. 'Hey, if I'm going to beat peak-hour traffic I've really got to—' but I found myself mesmerised as Declan calmly pulled out an intestine and manually squeezed the shit out.

His housemate came home that night to find the place stinking like the set of *Salò* after we decided that the only way to make sure the innards were truly hygienic and, more importantly, reusable, was to boil them whole in a pot, like they were lobsters.

And that is the truest image of this time that I can think of. The two of us, standing in a Brunswick kitchen, smiling at each other, probably already hearing the applause, over our very own steaming pile of horseshit.

▼ ▼ ▼ ▼ ▼

'Give me your name.'

'Give me your name.'

I have no idea what's going on, I just see strangers staring at me, giving me a look I've never seen before. It takes a second to register but it's a look that asks, 'Why the fuck aren't you laughing?' I didn't recognise it because I'm always the one giving that look. Because I'm always laughing.

'Give me your name.'

I look down. I'm sitting on a cheap black folding chair. The metal is rusted and covered in dust. In fact, everything seems to be covered in dust. I seem to be in a dark … place with strangers staring at me, asking me my name. And—I know that face, that's Declan, isn't it?

'Give me your name.'

And I think, 'Don't you know my name? We know each other, right?' Of course we do, of course we do. He must mean something else and so I think, 'Give me your name, give me your name.' Where have I heard this before? It must be from something, I mean everything we say to each other is from something but … what? And the only time I can remember someone actually saying those words, 'Give me your name,' is back in that Nimbus when Mum was driving Erin and I somewhere after school one day and there were these boys on bikes in front of the car. They kept crossing back and forth, refusing to let Mum pass. This is as close as you get to a bikie gang in Brighton. And when Mum politely but firmly honked the horn, instead of moving out of the way, one of the boys just turned around and—

ASH *sticks his middle finger up.*

And it—was—on. Heather puts her pedal to the metal, the Nimbus is now flying through the backstreets of Bayside and these boys are shit-scared because a family wagon is hurtling towards them and it shows no signs of slowing down. And Heather Flanders is not afraid to run down a child, okay? Only a year earlier I'd tried to run away from home by taking off down the laneway next to our house. I didn't even make it to the next street before she'd mowed me down, picked me up, slapped me across the face and made me apologise for scaring *her*.

The three boys have now split up thinking that'll make Mum lose interest but it has the exact opposite effect. It just makes the one she wants—the bold one with the finger—that much more vulnerable. Because if you bring it to Heather she'll finish it. If you start it, it ends with her. 'End of.' It's not just her catchphrase, it's her entire life philosophy. Which is why she is speeding through suburban streets, ignoring every stop sign until we finally land in a cul-de-sac. And this is mystifying to Erin and I because our mother has a terrifyingly bad sense of direction. I mean, we have lost entire days trying to find this very Nimbus in the Southland car park but she has herded this boy to a dead end on pure instinct alone, like a wolf with a lamb.

She winds down the window. 'Give me your name.'

'I'm sorry, all right? I didn't mean—'

'Give me your name.'

The kid tries to act tough but as Mum moves to get out of the car he gives up his name like that. Without so much as a prompt he gives up the names of his accomplices. Mum sits back in her chair, the engine purring—she was never getting out of the car—'I know that school uniform, and now I know your name. So when I speak to your principal tomorrow—and I will speak to your principal tomorrow—I better not find out you lied to me because then I'll be really annoyed. Last chance—give me your name.'

The look on the kid's face says he didn't even know lying was an option. He repeats the same name before politely asking if he may be dismissed.

'Get out of my sight.'

And as the kid tears off down the road Mum turns back to Erin and I, beaming with pride and awaiting her applause. Only, we're quite upset because we rightfully thought we were going to die many, many times, and for what—because some stranger flipped her the bird? But she doesn't notice. She's too busy bathing in the afterglow of the hunt, the kill. And I say to her, 'Mum, please, okay, I'm begging you. Please don't embarrass me. Promise me you're not going to go to that school.' And now she looks at me like I'm the lunatic, 'What? Of course I'm not going to the school. How much time do you kids think I have?'

'Well then why did you … ?' And that's when she exhales a cigarette I didn't even know she'd lit, the smoke pouring out her nostrils like a dragon, her favourite animal. 'I just wanted to scare him.'

'Give me your name!' Declan is now screaming these words at me and I go, 'What? What? Give me your'—but as I say it out loud it kicks in a muscle memory and I instantly remember we've been saying this for months. We've been saying, 'Give me your name,' in this haughty, John Watersy voice. You know, an outraged, indignant, 'Give me your name!' And we've laughed about it. We wrote the show we just closed while saying it. We said it throughout rehearsals. We made the whole cast say it and now—now this thing means nothing to me? This thing that has made me laugh for months is—is dead?

And I say, 'Is that it? Is that the joke?'

'Yeah. Ash, why aren't you laughing?'

And that's when I know the acid I took earlier has definitely kicked in. It's 2008, it's the closing night of our sexploitation comedy *Cellblock Booty* and I have just taken acid for the first time—twice—at the cast party held in our theatre, which is actually a car-park-slash-garbage-dump underneath government housing in Collingwood, where we have illegally locked ourselves in for the night.

And I no longer have a sense of humour.

I am a total stranger to myself.

Within the hour I'm hiding in the garbage with Jenni. She's my best mate, my housemate and my castmate and right now we are clearly having two very different trips. For me, it's a feeling of primal dread. I cannot laugh, I cannot smile, the world is violence and all I know for sure is I will die tonight. But Jenni's feeling a little different, she's weirdly dreamy and confessional. She's having a fabulous time, as she always does.

'Do you know,when you say something funny you actually, like, mouth it to yourself afterwards? It's true. You do it on stage too. In fact tonight in the—'

'Shut the fuck up!!'

I cover her mouth with my hand because I see something in the distance. A yellow light that's getting closer and closer. And I know it's a torch, I know it's a torch, I know it's just some guy with a torch. But it is also definitely the eye of a creature that will devour us if we're discovered.

Its voice calls out from the dark. 'Where are you? Where are you? I'm going to find you.'

And then the light—the eye—the torch—moves and I'm knocked to the floor. And I look up to see John, the only person at this party I don't trust because John is a drug dealer and I don't trust drug dealers even though I wanted John here because he is a drug dealer because I wanted to try acid for the first time. And even though it was John who said, 'Don't have that second hit of acid, Ash, it hasn't had time to kick in yet,' I know this has all been part of some sick conspiracy and now I know Jenni is in on it too.

I put a hand to my head and feel a sticky wetness. Sure enough, I'm bleeding. I've got blood on the brain. I'm going to die. And as Jenni and John start dancing or pashing or fucking in the trash I try and find a quiet place to die.

I land in prison. No, not prison, just the set of the women in prison show we closed tonight. But I'm lying in a prison bed holding a bloodied hand to my bloodied head and knowing now that I am crazy. I'm crazy. I'm never coming back from this. I had a brain once. I could write a play. All my thoughts went gently flowing down a river all in one direction but now the dam has burst and everything's underwater and I'm going to be stuck in this prison, in this car park, in this madness forever. And I cry. I cry the bitter tears of the mad because now I'm just like all those other people that never found their way back. Like the skinny guy I see at the train station every morning who rocks back and forth like he's about to jump. I'm him now. And I can see the train, a light that gets brighter and brighter and any second now I'm going to feel the rush as my body gets sucked under.

'Ooooooh.'

It's Declan. And that wasn't a train at all, it was just one of the floodlights from the show. He's over at the lighting desk, hunched over it like some weird bird.

'It's like a womb. It's like a womb. What do you need? What do you need right now?'

I need for everything to stop so I tell him to turn the lights off. But when he does I'm assaulted by images of everyone I know dying. Of war, of famines, of fires, of earthquakes, tidal waves, of faces on fire, screaming, laughing. 'Turn the lights back on!' But when he does it's worse because now I know this is real and this is all actually happening. I'm legitimately actually really actually crazy.

And I make my way over to the bird man. 'Hey, man. I'm not okay. I—I—I need help.'

And that's when the creature unveils its true form. It's not a bird at all. It's a grinning jackal. It's the Devil himself in a pair of black skinny jeans and a mesh top. He looks at me with his cold dead eyes and says, 'You're outside of time.'

'How do I get back?'

'It's simple, Ashleigh. You just need to remember who are your friends and who are your enemies.'

And with that—I swear to God he does this—he does a full Nosferatu pose and hovers back into the darkness from whence he came. My writing partner, my best friend, the bird, the jackal, the Devil. And I stand there, outside of time, for seconds or years before I finally understand the Devil's words. I need to be with my friends. They'll help me. They're just over there. But then a voice louder than my own says, 'They're not your friends! They can't stand you. Your desperate need to be seen. How amusing you find yourself. How everything is just ONE BIG JOKE TO YOU. They hate you! Listen to them laugh!' And they are laughing. And so I try and paint a smile on my face, try and force a laugh out so I can walk over like, 'I'm fine!' Like, 'I'm still me!'

And then I hear a new voice. No, voices.

'Help us. Save us.' It's the children. They need my help. The children need me. I'm all they've got.

And my new quest has me walking down further, deeper, darker, into the belly of the beast. This car park is huge when your brain is functional but when you're tripping this hard it's like you're crossing the Nullabor. I walk alone, outside of time, in the dark, listening only to the voices of children, the children only I can hear. And I land in this weird side annex that we've never really been in before. It was once artist studios but now it's just a bigger garbage dump, this one exposed to the elements. It hasn't rained for months but the garbage here is always wet, like the place is digesting itself. It's filthy and I'm deep inside it, tearing past mouldy food, fetid mattresses and rat shit trying to find the children, my children, my babies.

But they've stopped talking.

I was too late.

I lie down in the sopping filth and find myself staring into the eyes of a … rooster? A large papier-mâché creature that some artist has abandoned. We are immediately sisters. I nestle into it, I close my eyes and I wait to join my dead children. I open them when I hear the sound of water. Oh God, is it raining? No, the water's coming from Matt. I last saw him an hour ago, when he asked if I was okay and I'd snapped at him, knowing his concern was just another ploy to humiliate me. The water's coming from Matt, he's pissing into a drain. But it isn't a regular piss. I watch as a fluorescent lime-green torrent comes from Matt. In the moonlight streaming in from the grate above, a toxic green river pours out of Matt's sternum starting just below his neck and going all the way to his knees.

Matt pissing is the most beautiful thing I have ever seen in my life and it's this image that convinces me to join the real world again. So I crawl to the door of the car park and without saying goodbye to anyone I unlock it and find myself in Collinwood where I flag down a taxi. 'Please, take me home!'

And as the driver makes his way towards Windsor I know he's going to fuck me. I know he's going to leave me for dead. As the car tilts up the hill of Punt Road, I'm instantly aware we're about to drive off the edge of the world.

But we don't. He drives me home. He doesn't fuck me—I can't imagine why—and I find myself plagued by all new fears.

Oh God, please let me have cab fare. I do.

Oh God, please let me have my keys. I do.

Oh God, please let me know how to use keys.

And for the next five hours, this is all I do. Pray. To a God I don't believe in, seeing death every time I close my eyes.

▼ ▼ ▼ ▼ ▼

My first real experience of death was my dad's mum's passing. I don't remember a lot from that night. This isn't because it was so harrowing I've had to repress it but because it was such a typical Flanders family affair. It was all practicalities and no theatrics whatsoever—a real waste. A babysitter was called out of the blue, my siblings and I were told nothing, we just thought Mum and Dad were going to another work function. But the next morning, over breakfast, we were calmly told, 'Nana Flanders has died of acute angina.' Mum's look told me that, yes, there is a joke to be made, but we'll do it in private later. And we did. Dad didn't hold us close, he didn't cry, he didn't tell us everything's still going to be all right. To be honest with you I'd felt more afraid the night he'd told us in hushed tones about the recession. Nana Flanders was gone, simple as that.

But when Mum's mum died it was a very different story. We were at the house in seconds, the one Grandma shared with Aunty Sharon and the cousins. Everyone was there, drinking, smoking, crying and there was already a rumour that Uncle Nelson, who lived an hour away, had woken up with heart palpitations at the exact same time Grandma died of her heart attack. Yeah, bad hearts on both sides of the family. Drinking too. Both grandmothers died at sixty-nine just as Mum was planning their seventieth birthdays—quite rightly she took it personally. My grandfathers died before I was born or relatively soon after. As you can probably tell by now, heterosexual men rarely earn a place in my stories, or my memories. One was a drunk and one was a drunk and a poet and painter and a racist. I'll let you decide which one was from the Irish side.

I'd only known Mum's mum, Hallie, for a couple of years, really. She'd been catatonic most of our lives. The only move you'd see Grandma make was lighting another cigarette as she sat in her deep black leather chair, staring at you through the smoke as though she were trying to remember who you were … or how you got in. But two years before her death they changed her medication and it was like something out of that film *Awakenings*. Suddenly Grandma was leaping out of her chair to greet you at the door with a bear hug and a handshake that hurt even more than the whisker burn you'd feel after she kissed you.

See, say what you want about the Irish—the Irish do death well. And not just the wake—although even I tapped into my Irish lunacy that day and locked myself in a bathroom to cry alone, desperately hoping someone would notice—they didn't, they were all in their own bathrooms staging their own shows. But the Irish do the drama of dying well. See, Grandma's death was so much more tragic because it was as if she'd just started living again. She'd quit smoking even though tests had proven this lifelong addict still had the lungs of a thirteen-year-old girl. Although that, like Uncle Nelson's heart palpitation, could just be more Irish poetic nonsense. Everything on that side of the family is high stakes, magical and theatrical. She's been dead over twenty years now and I only just found out her name wasn't Hallie at all, it was Martha. These people take stage names. As they lowered her coffin into the plot she shared with her husband, Mum turned to the congregation and said 'Dad'll be furious, Mum's on top forever now', and we all laughed. That was how we said goodbye.

But the Flanders abstain from theatrics. If you see my father watching my mother you'll understand some people are just passionate about being a good audience. Although, Nana Flanders did pull one great stunt. After the service, Dad organised the cremation and it took a couple of weeks to get his brother's side of the family over to scatter the ashes. And for those interim weeks I would sneak into his study and stare up at the white, nondescript box where Nana was, feverishly trying to feel something while knocking back tonic water from the bar fridge because, 'No, mixers are the only soft drinks allowed in this house, end of.'

Finally, we were all gathered together at the rocks at the beach opposite our house. This was it. The big goodbye. But when Dad opened the box he found, not ashes, but another white, nondescript box, this one full of ashes. Only, it had the wrong name on it.

And looking back on it, what sticks out most is just how quickly we went from being a family united in quiet, dignified grief, to— well, an angry mob. Turns out there is a little fire in the Flanders clan after all but it's reserved for important things like clerical error. Dad marched back to the house to call up the crematorium. I, ever the hostess, offered everyone some tonic water. Dad came out ten minutes later and said, 'It's fine, turns out there were two people with the same surname cremated on the same day. The remains are right, it's just the label that's wrong.'

'It's … it's definitely Mum,' he said to Uncle Ian and even at eight I remember thinking, 'Well, of course they'd say that. What else were they going to say?'

It was a weak lie, and one I don't think either son actually believed. But while the Irish would have wept whiskey and howled for justice, the Flanders men simply took it in their stride, walked back to the rocks and released ... someone. Maybe it was their mother. Maybe it was a Dalmatian. Maybe it was a convicted felon. But at this point what did it really matter?

▼ ▼ ▼ ▼ ▼

'But do you actually want to live?'

It's 2019 and I'm at a café on Hampton Street that used to be a Browns Patisserie, where I'd applied for a job soon after drama school. 'You know, Lisa McCune comes in here—a lot,' the manager dropped casually and deliberately mid-interview. The whole thing went fine until she asked if I had any questions and I enquired about my hourly rate. 'Oh, it's twelve dollars an hour, do you have any other questions?' 'No,' I said, getting up, 'because I won't be working here.' In another time and place that might have sounded impressive or self-assured but back then I was just another Bayside son post-university: lost, hungry, but still deeply entitled.

'But do you actually want to live?' I ask my mother. The café is now stripped of its faux-French atmosphere and is a stark white box full of highly curated indoor plants, serif menus and gorgeous soft blond wood furnishings—the same gleaming ode to gentrification you can find in any city. Mum's arms were bruised from another fall and she complained about feeling foggy. She'd talked earlier about her new walker and how it meant she could now get out of bed and move around a bit more. It was parked at the same window I'd sat at for that job interview. And as I waited for her to answer a question I didn't know I'd be asking that day, I'd have given anything to talk about something else. Even Lisa McCune.

Two weeks later Dad and Erin finally took the big trip to Machu Picchu they'd been talking about for years. I kept referring to it as their honeymoon which, honestly, only Erin seemed to have a problem with. The real problem, as always, was Mother. Being left to her own devices at this point could be tricky, the woman's reckless, rich and has nothing to lose. She'd started a kitchen fire only weeks earlier when, while frying up some ghee, she'd taken her private elevator downstairs to hunt for cardamom pods. Yes, that's a lot to unpack. Which is exactly what I imagined the workers at The Mayflower, Brighton's premier aged-care facility, would be saying when Heather Flanders' luggage arrived for her four weeks of respite care!

Now, I haven't spent a lot of time in old folks' homes. Like I said, my grandparents had the decency to die suddenly so as to not bother a soul. According to my mother, even her childhood dog had been thoughtful like this. One night they saw it digging a hole, something it had never done before, only to be found the next morning lying in it, dead. 'He didn't want to bother us,' she'd say tearfully while refusing to heed the lesson.

But here I am, sitting in the built-in café of The Mayflower with Heather Flanders. There was a time prestigious families boasted of their arrival on the Mayflower, now they quietly sail out on it. In terms of a place to spend your twilight years, you could do a lot worse—and I'm confident I will. At The Mayflower there's a library, a formal dining room, a hairdresser's, even a cinema playing a film every two hours, although the day I looked every session was *Herbie: Fully Loaded*.

The café is perfectly named for its clientele of privileged Brighton boomers, Bossy Boots. Where the lattes are scalding hot and every pudding comes with ice cream AND cream. Mum went without the pudding, she was having her new favourite breakfast, salted porridge. 'No, you get used to it after a while.' I think she was pulling an Oliver Twist routine to really up the guilt we should feel for imprisoning her there.

'Oooh there's my boyfriend,' she said and I turned to see a man younger than me arriving and putting on an apron. I couldn't work out why he was her boyfriend until she said, 'He's the one that lets me sneak a bottle of wine back to my room. I JUST LOVE HIM!' So while my father is exploring the mysteries of the Incan Empire in Machu Picchu, my mother is essentially sneaking booze back to her cell. And as I went over to get her a fresh bottle of contraband, the boyfriend asked what name to charge it to. 'It's Gloria Flanders. Is that right?'

I only ever hear my mother's legal name in medical settings. She's always hated it. I do too. When people use it it means they don't really know her. I wonder if she felt the same whenever anyone called her mother Martha instead of Hallie. Gloria is not a terrible name. It means immortal glory. Heather? That's just a flower, evergreen, that thrives on barren land. I hear a crash and turn to see she's knocked a table with her walker, not that it's slowed her down. She's laughing at the shocked look on the old ladies' faces. I turn back to the boyfriend. 'Call her Heather.'

▼ ▼ ▼ ▼ ▼

It's very hard to tell when the health problems began. But when Dad did something no-one in our family had ever done before, turned seventy and survived, he celebrated by throwing an international spectacular, inviting each child and their partner to join him and Mum in Europe. We wondered how Mum would get on. She was walking less and less these days. But there I was in gorgeous Granada, Spain, with my equally gorgeous partner, Daniel—two homosexuals ridiculously spoiled on Dad's hard-earned money—and Mum couldn't walk more than ten steps without having to sit down. The pain in her back was so bad that the only Spanish activity Heather Flanders really took to on that trip was the siesta. So once she'd had her fill of tapas, and then pasta, and then crème brûlée—once those orthotics hit the tarmac at Tullamarine—she booked herself in for back surgery.

And, hey, we knew Mum had an addictive personality—the woman installed a poker machine in our house—but none of us thought you could get addicted to back surgery. But be warned! As soon as the first surgery, a mixture of fusing and bracing, failed to meet her expectations she insisted on a second one, this time right before another family trip, her seventieth. Two surgeries so close together runs a lot of risks, let alone if you plan on recovering in Australia's fanciest swamp, Port Douglas. So the surgeon made it clear in no uncertain terms, 'Heather, you can either have the surgery or you can have the trip but there is no way you're getting both.'

So once she got both we met her in Port Douglas where, to put it simply, she had lost her mind. Instead of ending every sentence with her trademark 'End of', she ended them with the similar but more troubling 'Endone'. And if you don't know, Endone is what we call Oxycontin here in Australia, it's medical heroin. Meanwhile, I've just come off a very divisive, experimental production of *Hedda Gabler*, killing myself both onstage and off, and here I was being beaten by mother yet again as she staged her one-woman, durational production of *Long Day's Journey Into Night*. And there really is nothing more entertaining than a seventy-year-old back-surgery patient falling off their chair at dinner again and again only to giggle as they're pulled back up to sitting. But I couldn't help but feel it was maybe one of those shows where the performer was enjoying it more than the audience.

A couple of days later we were back in Melbourne and I got a call from Dad. She'd had another fall out of bed, only this time when the ambulance got there she was rambling and incoherent. And that was the real scare because we've seen that woman knock back entire vineyards of Sauvignon Blanc and still be able to make a perfect stranger laugh or, more frequently, cry.

After some tests they discovered that she'd developed a potentially fatal staph infection from the second surgery—the one she'd insisted on. Now, staph is always hard to treat but it was further complicated by that fact it had now spread to the foreign material that was supporting her spine, where it might never be fully eradicated. She was on an antibiotic drip for months, she lost her appetite, she lost the ability to walk and she had quite possibly lost her mind.

Meanwhile, while that trauma would have been really useful for *Hedda Gabler*, it's kind of getting in the way of my latest gig—making people laugh at the Melbourne Theatre Company in a funny, silly solo show about a man who gets a job working in Barbra Streisand's basement.

One day before the show I decided to pay her a visit. As I entered her room I saw a nurse helping her back into bed. It felt private and diminishing so I snuck out and only entered again when I was sure the nurse was gone. I don't remember a lot of what we spoke about that day but when I went to leave she asked if I'd help with her pyjamas. She pulled herself up to sitting with the aid of a support pole next to the bed while I unfolded the top that Dad had brought in that day. And I thought that was all I had to do but when I looked back she'd raised her arms up in the air, a gesture I'd only ever seen small children perform. I saw her helpless and I saw her very vulnerable and at thirty-five I was struck dumb by the fact I'd never seen that before. And so I helped her into her pyjamas and I made sure she was comfortable and I got out of there as fast as I could, making up some excuse about needing to get to the theatre early.

And when I came out of the room I could feel my throat was hot and tight and my eyes were stinging. As I went for the elevator a nurse asked if I was all right and I felt even more ridiculous because there were people here saying actual final goodbyes. And I came out of the Epworth, the hospital where she'd had all her surgeries—a place I later heard referred to by a former nurse as 'the killing fields'—and started walking.

I walked for an hour and a half and when I looked up I'd walked to the wrong theatre. I didn't know what had drawn me there but outside I saw my friend Stephen sitting with some friends. And like a true actor I sat at that table and immediately monopolised it with my emotions, weeping in front of these people, one of whom I knew had lost a parent very early in life. The whole thing was selfish and greedy and embarrassing and necessary—like everything around a theatre always is.

And then I wiped my face and I went to work, doing the big, silly, funny, happy show she didn't get to see. That night as I opened the show with the first line, 'Memories, light the corners of my mind,' I looked out to see an elderly man already asleep. And perhaps for the only time in my life I kept doing the show for him instead of in spite of him.

▼ ▼ ▼ ▼ ▼

I'm sitting on a catamaran, staring out at the endless ocean in front of us. I'm in Greece, somewhere in the Ionian islands, sat on one of the two in-built stools at the front of the boat, watching as the blue water rushes beneath us. My mouth is open, my lips are dry and cracked and salty. I've just finished my second joint for the day. The sun is setting. And I'm staring into the gold of that sunset, a gold I don't think I've ever seen before. We've been out at sea all day and only now can I start to make out cliffs and trees and buildings far off in the distance. They're gold too. It's blinding.

And I begin to feel what can only be described as faith. It slowly builds within me, it spreads and swells within me. I feel giddy from it. I'm drunk on it. And as I stare into all that gold I start thinking of these lines by C. S. Lewis. Honestly, Christianity, it's more addictive than any drug. It's from the last book in his Narnia series, when all the worlds he built have collapsed and the children and the animals find themselves in a brand-new place. And all they can think to do is rush forward, to have more of this place, to be more of this place. 'Further up and further in' they say again and again as they sprint to the centre of all things. That's how I feel in this moment. I consciously understand how gods came out of this, how God came out of this—because how could all this beauty be by accident? There's too much of it.

And as we sail further into the gold the beauty only intensifies and I feel the waves get rougher. I feel myself lifting slightly out of the seat. I feel the thrilling soft lilt in my stomach like I'm on a rollercoaster. I feel the spray in my face. And I'm laughing. I'm laughing like a man possessed because all I have to do in this moment is just accept this beauty. Not comment on it, structure it or control it. Just let go and take it all in. If I can.

And I turn to my friend Ange on the other seat and I say, 'This is what life is about, Ange! It's about letting go! It's about acceptance and beauty and trust.' But even though she's sitting close to me, the roar of the ocean is too loud and she can't understand a word I'm saying. But I keep talking anyway. I tell her everything I'm learning in this moment. I talk about love and faith and energy and MY GOD, ANGE, I'M SO HIGH!

And then I turn to look at the ocean behind us and I see Costa, our skipper. He's exactly what you're imagining, only far, far hotter. He's further away than Ange, he's right at the back of the boat, up high smoking a joint and steering us towards all the gold. And he hasn't heard me. I mean, there's no way Costa could've heard a word I said. But he looks at me and he smiles knowingly and in a voice louder than the ocean he calls back, 'OF COURSE!'

▼ ▼ ▼ ▼ ▼

It was six a.m. when Jenni finally came home from the car park and I felt safe enough to sleep. At least, I assume that's what happened. All I know is that the next morning she thought we should eat something to straighten ourselves out. And we were standing on Chapel Street, getting a Banh Mi from N Tran Bakery when I made some comment about the night we'd had. Just some dumb throwaway line. But she laughed. And for the first time in my life I could feel my lips as they moved of their own accord, subconsciously filing that joke away with all the others. And it felt good to be back.

But sooner or later the reason I am the way that I am, the reason I am who I am, the one who actually GAVE ME MY NAME will be gone. Knowing her, she'll have the last laugh. We'll go to pull the plug only for her to wake up and say, 'You don't have the guts,' while she pulls it herself, cackling as she goes. When Dad had his heart operation a few years back—bad hearts—Mum's last words to him before he went under were, 'Don't head towards the fire.'

But even after the heart surgery that was successful, beating the staph, even after this latest back surgery which seems to be doing the job, nothing changes the fact that they too will be trotting off to the knackery sooner rather than later. And so I find myself taking note of everything they say, writing down every story word for word, obsessively making sure my transcript is perfect. As if by having it on paper I can stop time. Like I can push my foot down on the pedal and have the same moment again and again and again.

And it's the first thing you think about when they call you out of the blue or you get a text at a weird time. You think, like, this is it. This is it. This is the moment that the play that you've been watching—this world that they've built around you—is over.

Yeah.

And I wonder sometimes whether she'll come to me in psychic readings, in dreams, any time I smell a cigarette. It's hard to know what you'll hold on to when you believe in so little.

After Uncle Nelson died I asked Mum if she ever felt him with her. It was a sunny Spanish afternoon post-siesta and it was just the two of us, dangling our legs in the pool, drinking and listening to Dolly Parton. 'Not really,' she said. But there was this uncharacteristic waver to her voice, as if she didn't really believe what she was saying—I'd never heard it before.

So, like a cop to a suspect, I gave Heather Flanders a chance to amend her statement for the record I was keeping.

'So, Heather Flanders—at three-forty-three p.m.—just to confirm, do you think you'll see Nelson again when you die?'

This time she was sure.

'Fuck, I hope not.'

In spite of himself, ASH *starts laughing.*

He continues to laugh after the lights have faded out.

THE END

OUTRAGEOUS

CONFESSIONAL

UNEXPECTED

IFFIN THEATRE COMPANY PRESENTS

END OF.

RITTEN AND PERFORMED BY ASH FLANDERS

OCTOBER – 5 NOVEMBER 2022 | SBW STABLES THEATRE

RECTOR
EPHEN NICOLAZZO

SIGNER
THAN BURMEISTER

HTING DESIGNER
CHEL BURKE

SOUND DESIGNER
TOM BACKHAUS

STAGE MANAGER
JEN JACKSON

IFFIN
EATRE
MPANY

Government partners

NSW GOVERNMENT   Australian Government   Australia Council for the Arts

Griffin acknowledges the generosity of the
Seaborn, Broughton & Walford Foundation in
allowing it the use of the SBW Stables Theatre
rent free, less outgoings, since 1986.

BIOGRAPHIES

ASH FLANDERS
WRITER/PERFORMER
Ash Flanders is a multi-award-winning writer and performer based in Melbourne. He most recently wrote and starred in *SS Metaphor* (Malthouse Theatre), *Ash Flanders is Nothing* (Brunswick Ballroom) and *The Temple* (Malthouse Theatre). He created queer theatre company Sisters Grimm with Declan Greene, co-writing and performing in: for Malthouse Theatre/Sydney Theatre Company: *Calpurnia Descending*; for Melbourne Theatre Company: *Lilith: The Jungle Girl*; for MTC Neon: *The Sovereign Wife*; and for Sydney Theatre Company: *Little Mercy*. As an actor, Ash's credits include: for Belvoir: *Hedda*; for Little Ones Theatre: *Psycho Beach Party*; for Malthouse Theatre/ Sydney Theatre Company: *Blackie Blackie Brown*; and for Melbourne Theatre Company: *Buyer & Cellar*. His cabaret works have toured across the country and include *Meme Girls*, *Negative Energy Inc.*, *Playing to Win* and *Special Victim*. He has won several Green Room Awards and lost even more. He once lost a Helpmann award to Tennessee Williams and they haven't spoken since. He is very excited to present his latest play *This is Living* at Malthouse in 2023 and yes, television continues to prove elusive.

STEPHEN NICOLAZZO
DIRECTOR
Stephen is a Naarm-based theatremaker, director and co-founder of queer theatre company Little Ones Theatre. He is also Co-Artistic Director of Western Edge with Chanella Macri and John Marc Desengano. Recent credits include: for Griffin/La Mama: *The Happy Prince,* for which he won a Green Room Award for Best Director; for Griffin/Arts Centre Melbourne: *Merciless Gods*; for Belvoir/ Malthouse Theatre: *Looking for Alibrandi*; for Brisbane Festival/Joel Bray Dance: *Considerable Sexual Licence*; for Malthouse Theatre: *Loaded*; and for Melbourne Theatre Company: *Abigail's Party*. Stephen's other directing credits include: for Arts Centre Melbourne/Arts House/Brisbane Festival/Darwin Festival/Joel Bray Dance/ Liveworks/Perth Festival: *Daddy*; for Brisbane Festival/Rock Surfers/Theatre Works: *Psycho Beach Party*; for Brisbane Powerhouse/Darwin Festival/MTC Neon: *Dangerous Liaisons*; for Malthouse Theatre Helium: *Salome*; for MKA/Old Fitz: *sex.violence.blood. gore*; for Red Stitch Actors Theatre: *The Moors*, *Suddenly Last Summer*; for Theatre Works: *Dracula*; and for Token Entertainment National Tour: *Judith Lucy and Denise Scott's Still Here*. He has collaborated with Ash Flanders since 2012 on cabaret and contemporary performance work including: for Adelaide Cabaret Festival: *Special Victim*; for Arts Centre Melbourne: *Playing to Win*; for Brunswick Ballroom: *Ash Flanders is Nothing*; for Malthouse Theatre: *Meme Girls*; and for Theatre Works: *Negative Energy Inc.*. His productions have received 12 Green Room Award wins and a Sydney Theatre Award. Stephen was also the recipient of the Besen Family Artist Award in 2009 through Malthouse Theatre and was a member of the 2019 Lincoln Centre Theatre's Directors Lab (New York City). He is also a teaching artist for Victorian College of the Arts, COLLARTS, Monash University, and Melbourne Theatre Company Education.

NATHAN BURMEISTER
Designer

Nathan Burmeister is a Melbourne-based set and costume designer who works closely with new styles, forms, stories, and explores contemporary aesthetics and audience experiences. Nathan's recent works include: for Before Shot Productions: *Sneakyville*; for Bloomshed: *Animal Farm*; for Bloomshed/Darebin Arts Speakeasy: *Paradise Lost*; for Darebin Arts Speakeasy: *End Of.*; for Darebin Arts Speakeasy/Joel Bray Dance: *Considerable Sexual License*; for La Mama: *Q*; for Lyric Opera: *Fly*; and for Moral Panic/Theatre Works: *Love/Chamberlain*.

RACHEL BURKE
Lighting Designer

Rachel has an extensive and highly awarded body of work over three decades for main stage companies, independent theatre and architectural lighting design both nationally and internationally. Industry acknowledgment includes ten Green Room Awards for Theatre Lighting Design, IES Victorian and National Awards of Excellence for Lighting Design in 2005, 2010 and 2019 and Helpmann Award nominations in 2005 and 2015. Rachel held an academic position at Melbourne University/VCA Production and Design 2017–2019 and is Senior Associate at Relume Consulting. She is a graduate from Rusden Victoria College with a Bachelor of Education Secondary in Drama and Dance. Recent theatre design credits include: for Belvoir/Melbourne Theatre Company: *Sexual Misconduct of the Middle Classes*; for Kadimah Yiddish Theatre/Arts Centre Melbourne: *Yentl*; and for Red Stitch Actors Theatre: *The Amateurs*.

TOM BACKHAUS
Sound Designer

Tom is a freelance composer, sound designer and producer. As a sound designer he is known for his densely layered and evocative scores for theatre. A Music Technology graduate of the Queensland Conservatorium of Music, Tom draws upon his detailed understanding of music production, melding pre-recorded music and sound with live instrumentation to create dynamic and reactive scores. Some of his credits include: for Lab Kelpie: *Become the One*; for Melbourne Theatre Company: *Astroman*; for Malthouse Theatre: *The Importance of Being Ernest*, *The Temple*; for Red Stitch Actors Theatre: *The Feather in the Web*; for VIMH: *let bleeding girls lie*. In 2017, Tom was a recipient of the Besen Family Artist Placement at the Malthouse Theatre, working with Jethro Woodward on *The Real and Imagined History of the Elephant Man*. As a producer, Tom is best known for his work with drag comedy group Dazza and Keif. He has presented their debut work *Dazza and Keif Go Viral* in Adelaide, Melbourne (for which he was awarded Best Emerging Producer at the Melbourne Fringe Festival), Sydney and Wellington. In 2019 he presented the group's follow-up *Dazza and Keif Go Viral in Space with Ya Mum* at the Melbourne Fringe Festival along with a site-specific contemporary dance piece *Dark Points*. Tom also produces the queer festivalette, Get Bent Fest, showcasing LGBTQIA+ talent from Midsumma Festival and beyond.

JEN JACKSON
Stage manager

Jen Jackson (she/her) is a Korean-Australian stage manager, living and working on Gadigal land, with a particular passion for new Australian work and a commitment to diversity in theatre. After attending UNSW in a Bachelor of Arts majoring in Theatre & Performance, she continued her studies at NIDA with a degree in Technical Theatre & Stage Management. Recent productions she has stage managed include: for Griffin: *Golden Blood* (黃金血液); for Contemporary Asian Australian Performance: *Double Delicious*; for Kurinji/SAtheCollective: 宿 (*stay*); and for National Theatre of Parramatta: *Nothing*. Jen hopes to help bring to life stories of all kinds that challenge, entertain, reflect, make us feel, think, and examine ourselves—the kind of stuff that made her fall in love with theatre in the first place.

ABOUT GRIFFIN

Griffin is the only theatre company in the country exclusively devoted to the development and staging of new Australian writing. Located in the historic SBW Stables Theatre, nestled in the heart of Kings Cross, Griffin has been Australia's home for the exploration of new stories since 1978.

We are the launch pad for new plays, ideas and writing that other theatres won't take a risk on. We boldly contribute to Australia's unique and powerful storytelling culture. Plays like *Prima Facie*, *Holding the Man* and *City of Gold* all had their world premieres at Griffin before going out to capture the national imagination. In the words of our longest-serving Artistic Director, **Ros Horin**:

"We are the theatre of first chances."

We are passionate about nurturing emerging and established practitioners alike. We pride ourselves on supporting our vast community of artists, audiences and supporters who consider our theatre their creative home. We help ambitious, bold, risk-taking and urgent Australian work get from the page onto the stage. We tell the stories that help us know who we are as a nation, and who we want to become.

Acknowledgement of Country

Griffin Theatre Company and the SBW Stables Theatre operate and tell stories on the unceded lands of the Gadigal of the Eora Nation. We acknowledge and honour Aboriginal and Torres Strait Islander people as the oldest continuous living culture on the planet, with more than 60,000 years of storytelling practice shaping and underpinning all aspects of Australian culture. It is a privilege that we do not take lightly: to work on this land, and to tell stories on its soil.

GRIFFIN THEATRE COMPANY
13 Craigend St
Kings Cross NSW 2011

02 9332 1052
info@griffintheatre.com.au
griffintheatre.com.au

SBW STABLES THEATRE
10 Nimrod St
Kings Cross NSW 2011

BOOKINGS
griffintheatre.com.au
02 9361 3817

GRIFFIN FAMILY

Patron
Seaborn, Broughton &
Walford Foundation
*Griffin acknowledges the
generosity of the Seaborn,
Broughton & Walford
Foundation in allowing it
the use of the SBW Stables
Theatre rent free, less
outgoings, since 1986.*

Board
Bruce Meagher (Chair)
Guillaume Babille
Simon Burke AO
Lyndell Droga
Tim Duggan
Declan Greene
Julia Pincus
Lenore Robertson
Simone Whetton

Artistic Director & CEO
Declan Greene

Executive Director & CEO
Julieanne Campbell

Associate Artistic Director
Tessa Leong

Associate Artist
Andrea James

Literary Associate
Julian Larnach

Box Office Manager
Jackson Used

Ticketing Administrator
Nathan Harrison

Bar Manager
Alex Bryant-Smith

Front of House
Riordan Berry
Bridget Haberecht
Julian Larnach
Max Philips
Poppy Tidswell
Willo Young

Head of Development
Jake Shavikin

Relationships Manager
Ell Katte

Finance Manager
Kylie Richards

Finance Consultant
Emma Murphy

Marketing Manager (Acting)
Ang Collins

Marketing Assistant
Sasha Meaney

Production Manager
Jeremy Page

Deputy Production Manager
Ally Moon

Senior Producer
Imogen Gardam

Programs Producer
Janine Lau

**Ticketing & Administration
Coordinator**
Kate Marks

**Strategic Insights
Consultant**
Peter O'Connell

Sustainability Coordinators
Ang Collins, Julian Larnach

Brand & Graphic Design
Alphabet

Web Developer
DevQuoll

Cover Photography
Pia Johnson

GRIFFIN DONORS

Income from Griffin activities covers less than 40% of our operating costs—leaving an ever-increasing gap for us to fill through government funding, sponsorship and the generosity of our individual supporters. Your support helps us bridge the gap and keep ticket prices affordable and our work at its best. To make a donation and a difference, contact Griffin on **9332 1052** or donate online at **griffintheatre.com.au**

PROGRAM PATRONS

Griffin Ambassadors
Robertson Foundation

Griffin Amplify
Girgensohn Foundation

Griffin Studio
Gil Appleton
Darin Cooper Foundation
Kiong Lee & Richard Funston
Rosemary Hannah &
Lynette Preston
Ken & Lilian Horler
Malcolm Robertson
Foundation
Pip Rath & Wayne Lonergan
Geoff & Wendy Simpson OAM
Danielle Smith &
Sean Carmody

Griffin Studio Workshop
Mary Ann Rolfe (Patron)
Iolanda Capodano &
Juergen Krufczyk
Darin Cooper Foundation
Bob & Chris Ernst
Susan MacKinnon
Pip Rath & Wayne Lonergan
Walking up the Hill
Foundation

Griffin Women's Initiative
Katrina Barter
Wendy Blacklock
Jessica Block
Christy Boyce & Madeleine
Beaumont
Julieanne Campbell
Iolanda Capodanno
Laura Crennan
Jennifer Darin
Lyndell Droga
Judith Fox & Yvonne Stewart
Melinda Graham

Sherry Gregory
Rosemary Hannah & Lynette
Preston
Antonia Haralambis
Ann Johnson
Roanne Knox
Susan MacKinnon
Julia Pincus
Ruth Ritchie
Lenore Robertson
Deanne Weir
Simone Whetton
Green Griffin
Iolanda Capodano &
Juergen Krufczyk
Natalie Lopes
Amy Morcom
Alex-Oonagh Redmond

SEASON PATRONS
*As a new writing theatre,
we program a wide range of
stories that reflect our time,
place and the unique voice
of contemporary Australia.
To ensure that these stories
continue to be told, Griffin
needs the help of private
support to bring strength,
insight, candour and new
and powerful visions to
the stage. Our Production
Partner program is vital to our
continued artistic success.*

**PRODUCTION PARTNERS
2022**

**Whitefella Yella Tree by
Dylan Van Den Berg**

Lisa Barker & Don Russell
Darin Cooper Foundation
Robert Dick & Erin Shiel
Lyndell & Daniel Droga

Danny Gilbert AM &
Kathleen Gilbert
Rosemary Hannah &
Lynette Preston
Bruce Meagher &
Greg Waters
Richard McHugh &
Kate Morgan
Julia Pincus & Ian Learmonth
Pip Rath & Wayne Lonergan

SEASON DONORS
Company Patron $100,000+
Neilson Foundation

Season Patron $50,000+
Girgensohn Foundation
Robertson Foundation

Mainstage Donors $20,000+
Anonymous (1)
Darin Cooper Foundation
Robert Dick & Erin Shiel
Rosemary Hannah &
Lynette Preston
Julia Pincus & Ian Learmonth
Mary Ann Rolfe

Production Donors $10,000+
Lisa Barker & Don Russell
Gordon & Marie Esden
Abraham & Helen James
Ingrid Kaiser
Richard McHugh &
Kate Morgan
Bruce Meagher &
Greg Waters
Tim Minchin
Peter & Dianne O'Connell
Pip Rath & Wayne Lonergan
The WeirAnderson
Foundation
Kim Williams AM &
Catherine Dovey

GRIFFIN DONORS

Rehearsal Donors
$5,000 - $9,999
Anonymous (1)
Antoinette Albert
Gil Appleton
Wendy Blacklock
Ellen Borda
Susan Carleton
Bernard Coles
Ian Dickson
Lyndell & Daniel Droga
Danny Gilbert AM &
Kathleen Gilbert
Libby Higgin
Ken & Lilian Horler
Lambert Bridge Foundation
Kiong Lee & Richard Funston
Lee Lewis & Brett Boardman
Rosemary Lucas &
Robert Yuen
Sophie McCarthy &
Antony Green
Catriona Morgan-Hunn
Anthony Paull
Rebel Penfold-Russell OAM
Geoff & Wendy Simpson OAM
The Sky Foundation
Merilyn Sleigh & Raoul
de Ferranti
Danielle Smith &
Sean Carmody
Walking Up the Hill
Foundation

Final Draft Donors
$3,000-$4,999
Bob & Chris Ernst
Jocelyn Goyen
Sherry Gregory
James Hartwright &
 Kerrin D'Arcy
Roanne & John Knox
Don & Leslie Parsonage
Leslie Stern

Workshop Donors
$1,000-$2,999
Anonymous (6)
Baly Douglass Foundation
Katrina Barter

Helen Bauer &
Helen Lynch AM
Cherry & Peter Best
Jessica Block
Christy Boyce &
 Madeleine Beaumont
Dr Bernadette Brennan
Anne Britton
Corinne & Bryan
Stephen & Annabelle Burley
Iolanda Capodano &
Juergen Krufczyk
Julieanne Campbell
Louise Christie
Anna Cleary
Bryony & Tim Cox
Sally Crawford
Laura Crennan
Cris Croker & David West
Ros & Paul Espie
Brian Everingham
Jan Ewert
John & Libby Fairfax
Sandra Forbes
Jennifer Giles
Nicky Gluyas
Melinda Graham
Peter Gray & Helen Thwaites
Antonia Haralambis
Kate Harrison
John Head
Mark Hopkinson &
Michelle Opie
Michael Jackson
Ann Johnson
David & Adrienne Kitching
Elizabeth Laverty
Benjamin Law
Richard & Elizabeth Longes
Kyrsty Macdonald &
Christopher Hazell
Susan MacKinnon
Prudence Manrique
Lorin Muhlmann
Ian Neuss & Penny Young
David Nguyen
Shaan Perera
Ian Phipps
Martin Portus

Annabel Ritchie
In memory of
Katherine Robertson
Sylvia Rosenblum
Jann Skinner
Stuart Thomas
Elizabeth Thompson
Mike Thompson
Sue Thomson
Janet Wahlquist
Richard Weinstein &
Richard Benedict
Simone Whetton
Rob White & Lisa Hamilton
Rosemary White
Paul & Jennifer Winch
Elizabeth Wing

Reading Donors $500-$999
Anonymous (3)
Brian Abel
Priscilla Adey
Jane Albert
Amity Alexander
Wendy Ashton
Robyn Ayres
Melissa Ball
Phillip Black
Larry Boyd & Barbara
Caine AM
Tim Capelin
Michael Diamond AM MBE
Max Dingle OAM
Elizabeth Diprose
David Earp
Leonie Flannery
Alan Froude & David Round
Peter Graves
Erica Gray
Stephanie & Andrew Harrison
David Hoskins &
Paul McKnight
Sylvia Hrovatin
Nicki Jam
Mira Joksovic
Matt Jones & Rebecca
Bourne Jones
Colleen Mary Kane
Susan J Kath

GRIFFIN DONORS

Patricia Lynch
Ian & Elizabeth MacDonald
Suzanne & Anthony Maple-Brown
Robert Marks
Chris Marrable & Kate Richardson
Simon Marrable & Anna Kasper
Christopher Matthies
Christopher McCabe
John McCallum & Jenny Nicholls
Daniela McMurdo
Jacqui Mercer
John Mitchell
Neville Mitchell
Keith Moynihan
Patricia Novikoff
Carolyn Penfold
Belinda Piggott & David Ojerholm
Virginia Pursell
Alex-Oonagh Redmond
Karen Rodgers & Bill Harris
Gemma Rygate
Rob & Rae Spence
Mary Stollery & Eric Dole
Catherine Sullivan & Alexandra Bowen
Ariadne Vromen
Robyn Fortescue & Rosie Wagstaff
Helen Wicker

First Draft Donors
$200-$499

Anonymous (11)
Susan Ambler
Elizabeth Antonievich
William Armitage
Chris Baker
Jan Barr
John Bell AO, OBE
Edwina Birch
Andrew Bowmer
Peter Brown
Wendy Buswell
Ruth Campbell

David Caulfield
Amanda Clark
Sue Clark
Louise Costanzo
Brendan Crotty & Darryl Toohey
Bryan Cutler
Sue Donnelly
Peter Duerden
Anna Duggan
Kathy Esson
Elizabeth Evatt
Michael Eyers
Helen Ford
Judith Fox
Eva Gerber
Jock Given
Deane Golding
Keith Gow
Virginia & Kieran Greene
Jo Grisard
Edwina Guinness
Ruth Guss
Kate Haddock
Raewyn Harlock
Robert Henderson & Marijke Conrade
Grania Hickley
Matthew Huxtable
Marian & Nabeel Ibrahim
Andrew Inglis
James Landon-Smith
Penelope Latey
Liz Locke
Danielle Long
Norman Long
Noella Lopez
Maruschka Loupis
Anni MacDougall
Claire McCaughan
Louise McDonald
Duncan McKay
Paula McLean
Stephen McNamara
Anne Miehs
Julia Mitchell
Mark Mitchell
Sarah Mort

Margaret Murphy
Carolyn Newman
Suzanne Osmond
Catherine & Joshua Palmer
Peter Pezzutti
Christopher Powell
Janelle Prescott
Andrew Pringle
Dorothy & Adit Rao
Tracey Robson
Ann Rocca
Catherine Rothery
Kevin and Shirley Ryan
Dimity Scales
Julia Selby
Natalie Shea
Vivienne Skinner
Bridget Smith
Vanda & Martin Smith
Yvonne Stewart
Augusta Supple
Danny Tomic
Rachel Trigg
Samantha Turley
Adam Van Rooijen
Julie Whitfield
Eve Wynhausen
Robert Yuen
William Zappa

We would also like to thank Peter O'Connell for his expertise, guidance, and time.

CURRENT AS OF
19 SEPTEMBER 2022

SPONSORS

Griffin would like to thank the following:

OUR PARTNERS

Government Supporters

Benefactor

Australian Government
Australia Council for the Arts

NSW GOVERNMENT

CITYOFSYDNEY

S&W Foundation

Creative Partners

alphabet.

Brett Boardman Photography

COPYRIGHT AGENCY CULTURAL FUND

GIRGENSOHN FOUNDATION

MALCOLM ROBERTSON FOUNDATION

NEILSON FOUNDATION

paperjam PARTNERS

ROBERTSON FOUNDATION

Company Sponsors

Beppi's
Established 1956

bourke street bakery

CURRENCY PRESS

FOUR PILLARS
SMALL AUSTRALIAN DISTILLERY

MAR/QUE

P&V
WINE+LIQUOR
Merchants

Rosenfeld, Kant & Co.
Business & Financial Solutions

The Saturday Paper

SYDNEY BREWERY

THE UNIVERSITY OF SYDNEY

Griffin Theatre Company is assisted by the Australian Government through the Australia Council, its arts funding and advisory body; and the NSW Government through Create NSW.

ALSO FROM THE CURRENT THEATRE SERIES

DOGGED
Andrea James and Catherine Ryan
On the lands of alpine Victoria, on Gunaikurnai country, a story of familial bonds unfolds. Faced with the looming foreclosure of her family's property, a farmer's daughter is on the hunt in the rugged Australian bush—on territory that by rights isn't hers to travel through. From deep between the eucalypts, another woman—a mother dingo—searches desperately for her lost pups. She howls into the night, run ragged by hunger and grief. Over the course of one long night, the Woman and Dingo forge an alliance to claw closer to the things they ache for... but it's a dangerous deal to make.

Tumble down the dingo's den into a work of sheer Australian Gothic, brought to you by the collaborative collision of playwrights Andrea James (*Sunshine Super Girl*) and AWGIE-winner Catherine Ryan. *Dogged* is a bloody parable painted with electric movement and a story that stares you straight down the barrel.
978-1-76062-706-5

WHEREVER SHE WANDERS
Kendall Feaver

At one of Australia's oldest residential colleges, scandal is rare. Or, scandal that reaches the outside world anyway. Behind closed mahogany doors, there's always quiet money to mop up the mess. Writing the cheques this year is Jo Mulligan, the first female Master in the college's hundred-year history. And for Nikki Faletau— student resident and aspiring journalist—this is a time for hope, for change, for reform… That all changes when a serious allegation is made against a fellow resident. For Jo, it's a case of boys will be boys. For Nikki, it's yet another symptom of rape culture rearing its ugly head on campus.

Kendall Feaver (*The Almighty Sometimes*) started writing *Wherever She Wanders* when incidents of sexual misconduct were being flung into the unforgiving light of the internet. In 2021, the play has only become more prescient. Online, there are no rules: social media is polarising political discussion, comments sections are as concrete as they are chaotic, and many vulnerable people are getting caught in the crossfire of a debate raging out of any one person's control.

Like a 21st century reworking of *The First Stone*, this brilliant new work plunges into generational feminism's ever-growing divide with Feaver's signature ferocious wit.

978-1-76062-769-0

ORANGE THROWER
Kirsty Marillier
The night is still. The air is hot and thick. From up on the roof, matching houses stretch as far as the eye can see. Welcome to the sunny suburb or Paradise. While her folks are back in Johannesburg, Zadie is holding down the family fort. This means keeping her little sis away from bush doofs, avoiding the cute boy next door, and smiling when her nice white neighbours try to touch her hair. All that changes when an unexpected visitor bursts back into Zadie's life in the middle of the night, breaking the silence with loud music and even louder opinions. To make matters worse, someone's been pelting the house with oranges. All of a sudden, Zadie's got a big, sticky suburban mess on her hands.

Orange Thrower is the award-winning debut play from Kirsty Marillier. A fresh twist on the Australian coming-of-age story, this play is a joyful comedy, a curious mystery, and a poignant love letter to South African women.

978-1-76062-752-2

GOLDEN BLOOD
Merlynn Tong

Golden Blood by Merlynn Tong feels like a big-screen thriller, even though it's got a cast of two. Playing out on the neon streets of Singapore, it desperately claws back the extreme wealth it once knew, holding a rusty machete between its teeth. When her mother dies, a teenage girl is left alone within the four walls of the only thing she's inherited—a decaying penthouse in the heart of Singapore. To make matters worse, she's now in the care of her estranged brother, and he's not exactly up to the gig. For one, he's only a few years older than her. And two, he's a gangster. Like, an actual one.

Left with next to nothing, the orphaned siblings become a formidable, atypical corporation of two. But it's not long before cracks begin to show. What is the trade-off for desiring excessive levels of luxury? What should be kept in this world, and what should be offered to the next?

978-176062-751-5

GHOSTING THE PARTY
Melissa Bubnic

Coming home from her sister's funeral, Grace decides that at 87 years old … her time has come. She's done with it all. She's ready to leave the party. Her daughter, Dorothy, decides her mum is just depressed. She makes it her mission to show Grace the beauty of living. But Dorothy is divorced. Stuck in a dead-end job. Estranged from her own daughter, Suzie, who lives halfway across the world. Soon, Dorothy starts to worry that her mum might have the right idea.Pushing up daisies. Kicking the bucket. Ghosting the Party. The euphemisms are endless. For a phenomenon so certain and all-encompassing, humans are terribly good at looking for ways to avoid talking about death. It's easy to forget that the concept of 'checking out' can be complex, contradictory—funny, even. Especially when an old lady with a bone-dry wit is involved.

Three generations of women face brutal questions of mortality in this uproarious pitch-black comedy from Melissa Bubnic, internationally renowned writer of *Boys Will Be Boys* and *Beached*, with Griffin's Associate Artist Andrea James in the director's chair—hand on heart and tongue in cheek. Painted with poetry, unflinching honesty and an almost absurd amount of biting one-liners, confronting death has never been this (gravely) funny.

978-176062-775-1

WHITEFELLA YELLA TREE
Dylan Van Den Berg

Once in a blue moon, in the middle of nowhere, two teenage boys meet under a lemon tree. After a rough start, a fragile friendship fruits into a heady romance. Ty and Neddy fall madly in love, as teenagers are wont to do.If history would just unfurl a little differently, the boys might have a beautiful future ahead of them. But without knowing it, Ty and Neddy are poised on the brink of a world that is about to change forever. It's the early 19th century. Ty is River Mob. Neddy is Mountain Mob. And the earth they stand together on is about to be declared 'Australia'.

In his young career, Dylan Van Den Berg has won the Griffin Award, the Rodney Seaborn Playwrights Award, and the Nick Enright Prize for Playwriting at the NSW Premier's Literary Awards. In *Whitefella Yella Tree* he has penned a heart-warming and heartbreaking story about love, Country, and Blak queerness throughout history. Starring Helpmann Award-winner Guy Simon (*First Love is the Revolution*, *Wakefield*), and nurtured through the Griffin Studio program, *Whitefella Yella Tree* is a force of nature and a tender first kiss.

978-1-76062-784-3

www.ingramcontent.com/pod-product-compliance
Lightning Source LLC
Chambersburg PA
CBHW050028090426
42734CB00021B/3466